50 Conversation Classes

From ESLgames.com

Conversation topics

1 Age

2 Annoyances

3 Animals

4 Art

5 Birthdays

6 Books

7 Business

8 Cars

9 Clothes

10 Controversial opinions

11 Current affairs

12 Eating out

13 The environment

14 Fame

15 Food

16 The future

17 Getting to know each other

18 Halloween

19 Health

20 Holidays

21 Home

22 Humour

23 The internet

24 Jobs

25 Law

26 Love and marriage

27 Money

28 Movies

29 Music

30 Politics

31 School days

32 Shopping

33 Sleep

34 Sport

35 Technology

36 Television

37 Time

38 Towns and cities

39 Travel

40 The unexplained

41 The weather

42 Xmas

Grammar themed cards

43 Future with *will*

44 Past simple: childhood

45 Past simple: recent events

46 Present continuous

47 Present perfect: have you ever

48 Present perfect: life history

49 Present simple

50 Second conditional

Index of grammar bits

Introduction

The basis of a good conversation class is giving learners a reason and an opportunity to speak and scaffolding that speaking with lexis and grammatical structure as it is needed. The most fruitful conversations arise spontaneously and there is an art to listening well and asking the right questions to in order to uncover the nuggets of universal interest which provoke stimulating classroom discussion. However, some days we come up empty handed, maybe our learners are tired or reluctant to publicly speak up. Here it is also the teacher's role to give learners a gentle push into areas which hopefully will create intellectual arousal and thus opportunities for the teacher to support this output with appropriate input.

About the materials

The activities in this book are intended to facilitate and support rich and stimulating conversation and are *not* designed to produce standardised lessons. Each unit contains many possible branching off points which can be either pursued in more depth or accepted at face value.

How to use the material

Give a copy of the activity page to each learner and have them read the quote and give their reaction to it. Then put them into pairs or small groups to try and unscramble the *mixed up vocabulary* items. After about 10 minutes, go through the answers together.

Next have learners look at the *idioms and collocations* section. Feel free to go off-track as questions arise from the presented language. Maybe they have similar idioms in their own language, maybe they find the construction unusual or funny. Make it clear that it's not mandatory that learners are able to reproduce each of these idioms, but that understanding and inferring meaning is the main goal of the activity. If learners have questions about grammar you can address them in depth or stress that the main focus of this section is understanding and move on.

The *grammar bit* is deliberately located at the bottom of the page so it can be easily omitted from photocopies if you think it's unsuitable for the class. This section is not designed to lead into full grammar instruction but is intended to expose the student to a grammatical structure that might be useful in the conversational part of the lesson. This section also serves to reassure learners that explicit grammar learning is being represented

.

It is of course possible to segue into a longer, more structured grammar explanation at this (or any other) point if it feels appropriate. One way to work with the *grammar bit* is to have learners copy the grammatical structure but change the context - either through putting an example sentence on the board and having the class suggest transformations, or asking learners to create their own grammatically similar sentences either individually or in pairs.

The last part of the class is the free conversation stage. Give groups of learners a deck of shuffled question cards placed face down on the table in front of them. You may choose to pre-teach any vocabulary you think might be unfamiliar at this point, or alternatively let the groups attempt to uncover meaning for themselves (or ask for your help).

Learners take it in turns to turn over the top card and ask their question to the other group members. The questions should be asked to each member in turn in order to give everyone a chance to speak but spontaneous group discussion shouldn't be discouraged. Be on hand to take notes and help out where needed. Finally, when the conversations are dying out, or after a specified time limit, go over anything interesting you heard during the activity and ask groups what other information they found out during their conversations. Further discussion may well spring up again during this final stage.

1 Age

"My grandmother started walking five miles a day when she was sixty. She's ninety-seven now, and we don't know where the heck she is."
— Ellen DeGeneres

Mixed up vocabulary

coddhihol - (n) the time when you were young

tenrgeae - (n) someone aged between 13 and 19

piennerso - (n) someone who has finished their working life

mldeid-**a**dge - (adj) to be neither young nor old

mutaer - (adj) to behave like an adult, not like a child

rtreteienm - (n) the time after your working life has ended

tlddore - (n) a very young child

Idioms and collocations

Ben wants to be an archaeologist when he *grows* _____ .

He's *getting on a* _____ but he's still got a great voice.

You look *good for your* _____ , what's the secret?

The 1930s were the _____ *age* of Jazz.

Disneyland was fantastic, we had the _____ *of our lives* there.

up	*bit*	*age*	*time*	*golden*

Grammar bit

<u>If I could</u> retire tomorrow, <u>I would</u>. I would spend my time travelling around the world and learning about different cultures.

1 Age

What's the best age to be?	In your country how old must you be to smoke, drink, drive and get married?
How old were you when you left home?	What advice would you give to someone half your age?
What do you think is the best age to have children?	What do you think is the best age for a political leader?
What's the retirement age in your country?	Have you ever lied about your age?
Would you like to live until you were 1000?	Do you think a large age difference is unimportant in a relationship?

2 Annoyances

"People who think they know everything are a great annoyance to those of us who do."
— Isaac Asimov

Mixed up vocabulary

iierrtta - (v) to annoy someone

ptse - (n) someone or something which is annoying

incnnnoeveti - (adj) something unhelpful or problematic

fresatdrut - (adj) how you feel when you have trouble doing something

fiuorsu - (adj) very angry

bda doom - (n) the feeling you have when you are not happy

clam wond - (v) what you might say to someone who is feeling angry or annoyed

Idioms and collocations

The new traffic lights are a *pain in the* _____ .

My supervisor is *driving me* _____ today.

This weatherman *gets on my* _____ , he's always so jolly.

My boss *hit the* _____ when she found out about the missing money.

it really _____ *me* when you eat with your mouth open.

crazy	*bugs*	*neck*	*nerves*	*roof*

Grammar bit

I'm so <u>frustrated</u> by my English homework, English grammar is very <u>frustrating</u>, and the lesson was so <u>boring</u>, I've never been so <u>bored</u> in all my life.

2 Annoyances

What annoys you about the English language?	**Which celebrities annoy you?**
What annoys you about the town where you live?	**Do any of your friends or coworkers have annoying habits?**
Do you think you have any annoying habits?	**When you're getting annoyed do you bottle it up or let it out?**
What really makes you mad?	**Do you ever get annoyed with yourself?**
Do you ever get annoyed with inanimate objects?	**What annoying things do young or old people do?**

3 Animals

"The greatness of a nation and its moral progress can be judged by the way its animals are treated."
— Mahatma Gandhi

Mixed up vocabulary

vte - (n) a doctor who looks after animals

cllaor - (n) dogs often wear one of these around their necks

hteneibra - (v) some animals have a long sleep in the winter

prru - (v) cats do this when they're happy

mlmama - (n) animals that feed milk to their young (e.g. humans, cows, cats)

reetlip - (n) animals that have cold blood and lay eggs (e.g. snakes, lizards, turtles)

bkar - (v/n) the noise a dog makes

Idioms and collocations

She crept out *as quiet as a* _____, but the baby woke up and started crying.

John is the *black* _____ of the family. He's always in some kind of trouble.

This is a tough business. It's a *dog eat* _____ world.

I'm so hungry, I could *eat a* _____.

Who *let the* _____ *out of the bag* and told Ann about her surprise birthday party?

sheep	*horse*	*mouse*	*dog*	*cat*

Grammar bit

Ostriches can run almost <u>as fast as</u> lions and their kick is <u>as powerful as</u> a kangaroo's. However their brains are only <u>as big as</u> a walnut.

3 Animals

Do you like going to zoos?	**Do you have any pets?**
Have you ever been bitten or stung by an animal?	**Are you afraid of any animals?**
Have you ever thought about becoming vegetarian?	**What animals live in the wild in your country?**
Would you like to go hunting?	**Are you a cat person or a dog person?**
What animals have you seen in the wild?	**Do you think it's ok to wear fur?**

4 Art

"Football is an art, like dancing is an art - but only when it's well done does it become an art."

— Arsene Wenger

Mixed up vocabulary

pinta - (n) colourful liquid which is used to make pictures with

daniwgr - (n) a picture made with a pencil

gayller - (n) a place you go to see art

poitrart - (n) a painting or drawing of a person (usually only their head and shoulders)

mapierstece - (n) a great piece of art, the artist's best work

csvana - (n) the material a painting is painted on

teicnhque - (n) a special method which an artist may use

Idioms and collocations

A _____ *is worth a thousand words.*

Maybe he's nice, don't *judge a* _____ *by its cover.*

I'll give him one more chance but we have to *draw a* _____ somewhere.

It's my birthday so we're going out to *paint the* _____ *red.*

The boss didn't like it, so I'm afraid it's *back to the drawing* _____ .

board	picture	town	book	line

Grammar bit

The Mona Lisa <u>was painted</u> by Leonardo da Vinci in the 16th century. It <u>was stolen</u> from the Louvre in 1911, and it was another two years before the painting <u>was recovered</u> by police.

4 Art

What pictures do you have on your walls?	Have you seen any famous works of art?
Do you have any artistic talents?	Who's your favourite artist?
What kind of art do you like?	How often do you visit museums or art galleries?
Who are the most famous artists from your country?	What do you think of modern art?
Describe an interesting photograph you've seen?	Do you own any original pieces of art?

5 Birthdays

"You can't help getting older, but you don't have to get old."
— George Burns

Mixed up vocabulary

perstens - (n) what you hope to receive lots of on your birthday

ckea - (n) people often eat a piece of this on their birthday

cdnlaes - (n) there's one for every year and you have to blow them out and make a wish

gfti **v**uceohr - (n) it's like money, but you can only spend it in one particular shop

prtay - (n) your birthday is a good excuse to have one of these

susrripe - (n/adj) something unexpected and nice

bloanol - (n) there are often some of these at a child's birthday party

Idioms and collocations

In the UK you *come of* _____ on your 18th birthday.

Martin was the _____ *of the party*, he didn't stop dancing all night.

I hope you *have a* _____ at your party tonight.

Come on Mick! It's a party, *let your* _____ *down* and have a drink and a dance.

The test was really easy, it was a *piece of* _____ .

hair	cake	age	ball	life

Grammar bit

The party was <u>so great</u>, we had <u>such a fun time</u>. Tom was <u>so drunk</u> that he fell asleep on the sofa. I got <u>such a lot of presents,</u> and later the police came because the music was <u>so loud</u>.

5 Birthdays

Have you ever been invited to a surprise birthday party?	Do you share your birthday with anyone famous?
How many people's birthdays do you know off by heart?	What's your star sign? Does your personality match your star sign?
What did you do for your last birthday?	How would you spend your perfect birthday?
Have you ever celebrated your birthday in another country?	Do you know what time of day you were born?
How do people celebrate birthdays in your country?	Do you know anyone who has their birthday on or near a big celebration day?

6 Books

"We shouldn't teach great books; we should teach a love of reading."
— B.F. Skinner

Mixed up vocabulary

ctntnseo - (n) usually found at the front of a book, it tells you what is in the book

ctrphea - (n) books are often divided into these

potl - (n) what happens in a book, the story

pakcberpa - (n/adj) a book with a soft cover, not a hardback

ixden - (n) usually at the back of the book, this lists in detail what is in the book

smki - (v) to read something quickly in order to get a general idea of the content

nno-**f**niotic - (adj) a book about a real-life subject, not a work of fantasy

Idioms and collocations

I helped her move house at the weekend, so I'm *in her good* _____ .

The team completely *lost the* _____ after they let in the second goal.

Moving to New York was the start of *a new* _____ in my life.

I couldn't believe it either, but sometimes _____ *is stranger than fiction.*

Reading between the _____ , I don't think he's enthusiastic about the idea.

chapter	*books*	*plot*	*lines*	*truth*

Grammar bit

I think this book is very <u>underrated</u>. I was <u>overwhelmed</u> by this story about <u>underprivileged</u> children growing up during the industrial revolution.

6 Books

What was the last book you read?	If you don't like a book, do you still try to finish it?
Who is your favourite author?	What kind of books do you like to read?
Have you ever read a book that had a big effect on your life?	Do you have an eReader?
Do you sometimes reread your favourite books?	Can you judge a book by its cover?
Have you read a book that you thought was overrated?	How do you decide what books to read?

7 Business

"There are no secrets to success. It is the result of preparation, hard work, and learning from failure."
— Colin Powell

Mixed up vocabulary

mernakigt - (n) making people aware of a company and its products or services

mareagn - (n) a person who is in charge of a team, project or department

airvtdese - (v) you need to do this if you want people to know about a product

pfotri - (n) the money you have made after deducting your costs

lsso - (n) if you didn't make enough money, you probably made a _____

baker - **e**nev - (v) you do this if you don't make money or lose money

minegte - (n) a get-together with colleagues to discuss business matters

Idioms and collocations

I'm on holiday next week, but please *keep me in the* _____ while I'm away.

Joshua was late for the meeting again, so he can *take the* _____.

I'm going to have to work all weekend in order to *meet the* _____.

If we release it this quarter, I'm certain we can *corner the* _____ in smart-wallets.

That was Tom on the phone, we've *got the green* _____ to start the Omega project.

deadline	*light*	*market*	*loop*	*minutes*

Grammar bit

<u>If we lower</u> the price by $3, I think <u>we can increase</u> sales two-fold.

 - Yes. <u>If we sell</u> it for $9.99, <u>we'll definitely increase</u> sales, but <u>we won't make</u> as much profit.

7 Business

What's the biggest company in your country?	Have you ever worked for a really big company?
Are there any companies you would like to work for?	Do you have a business card?
Are there any state-owned businesses in your country?	Would you like to start your own company?
What kinds of businesses might have trouble surviving in the future?	Are there any companies you don't like but you have to use?
Are there any companies you wouldn't work for?	Do many people own stocks and shares in your country?

8 Cars

"Have you ever noticed that anybody driving slower than you is an idiot, and anyone going faster than you is a maniac?"
— George Carlin

Mixed up vocabulary

t**ffairc j**ma - (n) a lot of cars on the road, all going nowhere

berka - (n/v) you use this to slow the car down

reserve - (n/v) use this gear to go backwards

wincsedren - (n) it's made of glass and the driver looks through it

srepa t**r**ye - (n) you should keep one of these in the boot in case you get a flat

raod **s**nigs - (n) these tell you where you're going and how fast you can drive

egeinn - (n) the bigger this is, the faster the car

Idioms and collocations

This new log-in procedure is *driving me round the* _____ .

Ok, it's time to *change* _____ and practise some of this new grammar.

After eight hours of talks, negotiations seem to have come to a *dead* _____ .

Sandra, you're *in the driving* _____ on this project.

Fasten your _____ , things are about to get interesting.

seatbelt	end	bend	seat	gear

Grammar bit

The bigger the engine, the faster the car; the later you are, the more red traffic lights you hit; the faster you drive, the more petrol you will use.

8 Cars

Do you prefer to drive or to be a passenger?	Which classic car would you like to own?
Do you prefer sports cars or luxury cars?	What's the best car you've ever driven or had a ride in?
What do other car drivers do that makes you angry?	What's the most important factor when choosing a new car?
How do you think cars will develop in the next twenty years?	What was your first car?
Do you think there are too many cars on the road? What's the solution?	Did you pass your driving test the first time?

9 Clothes

Mixed up vocabulary

suti - (n) smart business clothes, usually worn by men

udnrreawe - (n) clothes which aren't usually visible

weodbrar - (n) a type of cupboard where you hang your clothes

thtgi - (adj) the opposite of loose, maybe you should get a bigger size

bygag - (adj) another word for loose clothing

palin - (adj) not striped, not patterned, not bright, just a single colour

hlese - on the bottom of your shoe, they can make you seem taller

Idioms and collocations

Oh no, not another meeting! The new Head of Sales *bores the* _____ *off me.*

Wow; look at you! You're *dressed to* _____ tonight.

Basically, he *got the* _____ from his last job because he was too lazy.

That was *below the* _____ , don't talk about my family like that .

Come on, there's still 250 to do, let's *roll up our* _____ and get on with it.

kill	*belt*	*sleeves*	*boot*	*pants*

Grammar bit

Well this jacket looks <u>nicer</u> than the last one, but the last one was <u>cheaper</u> and a <u>better</u> fit.

 - I think I prefer the first one, it's the <u>trendiest</u> and the <u>most comfortable</u>.

9 Clothes

Where do you like to shop for clothes?	Do you have a favourite item of clothing?
Where did you get the clothes you're wearing now?	Have you ever bought something quite expensive but only worn it once or twice?
What kind of clothes suit you?	Do you like to wear bright and colourful clothes?
Can you judge someone by the clothes that they wear?	Is there a dress code at your workplace?
Do you ever buy clothes online?	What is something that you would never wear?

10 Controversial opinions

"If an individual wants to be a leader and isn't controversial, that means he never stood for anything."
— Richard Nixon

Mixed up vocabulary

anmetrgu - (n) an emotional discussion

bna - (v/n) to forbid something or make it illegal

comipsrmoe - (n/v) to come to an agreement where neither side wins or loses

iuess - (n) the subject which is being discussed

abilosh - (v) to officially get rid of something such as a tax or a law

pinot **of v**iwe - (n) a person's perspective or opinion

dabtee - (v/n) a discussion where different opinions are expressed

Idioms and collocations

You're *on my* _____ , aren't you? You think the logo should be bigger too.

I spoke to Ian and we've *agreed to* _____ on the overtime issue.

I had a *heated* _____ with my boss, and I told him I was going to quit.

I am very different to my sister. We don't *see eye to* _____ *on* anything.

I'm *sitting on the* _____ on this one, I can see both points of view.

eye	*side*	*fence*	*differ*	*discussion*

Grammar bit

I think soft drugs <u>should be legalised</u> and as a result, a lot of prisoners <u>could be released</u> from jail.

 - No, I don't agree. Anti-drug laws <u>must be made</u> stricter, or there will be total chaos.

10 Controversial opinions

Cigarettes should be banned	Cannabis should be legalised
The internet should be regulated to protect children	Nobody should be allowed to earn more than $1,000,000 a year
English grammar is not important as long as people understand you	National Service should be introduced / abolished
Keeping animals in zoos is cruel	Children should learn about sex at school
Pirating movies and music isn't a big deal	Old or sick people should have the right to take their own lives

11 Current affairs

"People everywhere confuse what they read in newspapers with news."
— A. J. Liebling

Mixed up vocabulary

maedi - (n) television, radio, and the press are all examples of this

diatsesr - (n) a terrible event

entcoiel - (n) when people vote for something e.g. a new political leader

desotmtnioran - (n) people marching in the street to show their feelings about an issue

awdar **s**owh - (n) an event where prizes are given, for example the Oscars

tialrvi - (adj) the opposite of important

curto **c**eas - (n) a process which decides if a person is innocent or guilty of a crime

Idioms and collocations

Smith *hit the* _____ last year when he became the youngest athelete to win a gold medal.

Miguel *added fuel to the* _____ by accusing his former boss of taking bribes.

The recession has hit us hard, we're all *in the same* _____ in facing these cutbacks.

Only *once in a blue* _____ do these two teams meet in a competition.

Is Bitcoin *a flash in the* _____ or the future of money?

boat	headlines	moon	pan	boat

Grammar bit

Clark <u>said</u> that <u>he expected</u> to see the economy improve and <u>hoped</u> to have some good news to announce soon. He <u>promised</u> that <u>he would</u> do all that <u>he could</u> to improve the job situation.

11 Current affairs

Do you think it's important to stay up to date with current affairs?	**In your opinion, which are the best and worst newspapers?**
How do you get your news?	**What's the biggest story in the news at the moment?**
Do you think there will still be newspapers in five years?	**What annoys you about news reporting in your country?**
Have you ever been in a newspaper?	**What would you like to see more of in the news?**
What would you like to see less of in the news?	**What headline do you hope to see one day?**

12 Eating out

"When you go to a restaurant, the less you know about what happens in the kitchen, the more you enjoy your meal."
— Jeffrey Wright

Mixed up vocabulary

chkec - (n) in the US you ask for this at the end of a meal, in Britain they say *bill*

mnia **c**eruos - (n) this part of the meal follows the starter

revoretaisn - (n) you need to make one of these before visiting a popular restaurant

wlel **d**neo - (adj) one way of ordering your steak

vatargeeni - (n/adj) someone who doesn't eat meat

cruelty - (n) collective name for knives, forks, spoons, etc.

nipnak - (n) something you wipe your mouth with during or after a meal

Idioms and collocations

Put your money away. It's your birthday, so dinner is *my* _____ .

I can't eat all this food, please can you put it in a _____ *bag* for me?

I shouldn't have ordered the large portion, *my eyes were bigger than my* _____ .

I can't eat a single thing more, I'm *completely* _____ .

I have a *sweet* _____ , I can't resist dessert.

treat   belly   tooth   doggie   stuffed

Grammar bit

<u>If I'd known</u> the portions were so small, I <u>would've had</u> a bigger lunch.

 - Yes, and <u>if you'd read</u> the restaurant review <u>you would've known</u> that the portions here aren't very big.

12 Eating out

How often do you eat out?	How often do you get takeaway food?
What's your favourite restaurant?	How much do you usually tip?
Have you ever worked in a restaurant?	Do you prefer home cooked food or restaurant food?
What's your favourite dish?	Do you usually have a starter and a dessert when you go to a restaurant?
Have you ever eaten in a very expensive restaurant?	When you eat in a restaurant do you try something new or something you know you like?

13 The environment

"A nation that destroys its soils destroys itself. Forests are the lungs of our land, purifying the air and giving fresh strength to our people. "
— Franklin D. Roosevelt

Mixed up vocabulary

rani ftesor - (n) a dense area of trees, usually in places with a tropical climate

botctyo - (v/n) avoid buying a product or goods from a particular company

cosyuntdire - (n) not towns and cities

weldfili - (n) animals and vegetation in their natural environment

plnaet - (n) Earth is one of these and so are Mars, Saturn and Jupiter

ptlleou - (v) to make the environment unclean and poisonous

siclk - (n) a layer of oil floating on the surface of water

Idioms and collocations

I've been working on this for so long, I *can't see the* _____ *for the trees* anymore.

It wasn't me! It's *not in my* _____ to take people's things without asking.

Studies say 5% of under 14s are smokers, some fear that this is just *the tip of the*

_____ .

The pool cost him $100,000 to build, but for the millionaire businessman that's a

_____ *in the ocean.*

That's typical of the press, always trying to *make a mountain out of a* _____ .

wood   drop   iceberg   molehill   nature

Grammar bit

In my opinion most people are<u>n't</u> doing <u>enough</u> to reduce the amount of energy they use. They also use <u>too much</u> water and buy <u>too many</u> things that they don't really need.

13 The environment

What do you recycle?	How worried are you about global warming?
How do you try to save energy?	Have environmental concerns changed the way you travel?
Are you worried that we might run out of oil sometime soon?	How do environmental concerns influence what you buy?
Do you think new technologies might solve some of today's environmental problems?	What will future generations think about how we are treating the environment today?
What do you think about nuclear power?	Have you noticed changes in the climate in your lifetime?

14 Fame

"In the future everybody will be world famous for fifteen minutes."
— Andy Warhol

Mixed up vocabulary

clbteriye - (n) a famous person

rde **c**repat - (n) this is rolled out for VIPs to walk on

gopsis - (n/v) to talk about the personal life of other people

tabdoli - (n/adj) a newspaper which has a lot of trivial stories about famous people

stra - (n/v) a word which is used to describe very famous musicians and actors

guoraolusm - (adj) to be attractive, often in an expensive way

pimerree - (n/v) the first showing of a new movie

Idioms and collocations

I like Jack, he seems so *down to* _____ for a big movie star.

My *claim to* _____ is that I once met Madonna at a party.

I hate speaking in public, I get terrible _____ *fright.*

Manchester United's star player was *in the* _____ after scoring three goals.

Amy Texas made *front* _____ *news* last year when she won a Grammy for best song.

fame *stage* *spotlight* *earth* *page*

Grammar bit

<u>I've never met</u> anyone really famous. The most famous person <u>I've spoken</u> to is my cousin Joe who plays guitar in a rock band. They were on TV once. <u>I've never been</u> on TV, have you?

14 Fame

Who is the most famous person you've met or seen?	Who is the most famous person in the world?
Who is the most famous person from your country?	What would you like to be famous for?
What are the downsides of being famous?	What are the benefits of being famous?
If you could have dinner or a drink with any living person, who would you choose?	Which famous people living today might still be remembered in 100 years?
If you were rich and famous, how would you spend your time?	Which famous person would you be happy never to see again?

15 Food

"It's easy for Americans to forget that the food they eat doesn't magically appear on a supermarket shelf."
— Christopher Dodd

Mixed up vocabulary

nosuitrtiu - (adj) a way to describe healthy food

duoslicei - (adj) very tasty

froavlu - (n/v) vanilla, chocolate and strawberry are all different _____s of ice cream

bnadl - (adj) food which tastes boring is this

repcie - (n) a formula for making a particular meal

truxtee - (n) - how food feels in your mouth when you eat it

pnitroo - (n) the amount of food you are served

Idioms and collocations

Growing up is hard, life isn't always *a bowl of* _____ .

He walked in, *as cool as a* _____ , and told the boss he wanted a pay rise.

We're going to try using a _____ *and stick* approach with the development team.

I'm not a fan of free jazz, it's *not my cup of* _____ at all.

To put it *in a* _____ , you're fired!

cherries	nutshell	cucumber	carrot	tea

Grammar bit

I <u>prefer</u> Indian food <u>to</u> English food. I'd <u>rather have</u> a good spicy curry <u>than</u> boring old meat and potatoes.

15 Food

Are you a fussy eater?	Do you care where the food you eat comes from?
What national dishes from your country would you recommend?	What do you think of genetically-modified (GM) food?
How has your taste in food changed over time?	What are your guilty pleasures?
What was the last meal you cooked?	What's your perfect breakfast?
Is anyone in your family vegetarian?	How healthy is your diet?

16 The future

"I know not with what weapons World War III will be fought, but World War IV will be fought with sticks and stones."
— Albert Einstein

Mixed up vocabulary

rtobo - (n) a machine which operates without human control

perinditco - (n) a guess about a future event

frotune **t**erell - (n) a person who claims to be able to see into the future

fecoastr - (n/v) the outlook for the future (for example, *weather* _____)

utpioa - (n) a perfect world

apacployes - (n) the end of the world

brakergohuth - (n) an important discovery which allows progress to be made

Idioms and collocations

The iPhone was *ahead of its* _____ and revolutionised the industry.

If I *look into my crystal* _____ , I see a bleak future for newspaper journalism.

If I make an *educated* _____ , I think we'll see driverless cars within 10 to 15 years.

In the *short* _____ petrol prices will continue to rise.

Time will _____ if the Minister's growth forecasts are too pessimistic.

ball   time   term   tell   guess

Grammar bit

By the year 2020, mobile phones <u>will be</u> much smaller and thinner and <u>could have</u> a battery life as long as a week, you <u>should be</u> able to download a movie in just a few seconds.

16 The future

Would you like to live for 1000 years?	**What might your mobile phone be able to do in ten years time?**
Are you optimistic or pessimistic about the future?	**Would you like a car that drives itself?**
What possible future invention do you wish existed now?	**What do you think people will do for entertainment in the future?**
Do you think people will work more or less in the future?	**What could be some important political issues in the next decade?**
What laws do you think could change in the future?	**If it was possible to time-travel, which time period would you like to visit?**

17 Getting to know each other

"There are no strangers, only friends you have not met yet."
— W.B. Yeats

Mixed up vocabulary

seakh **h**snad - (v) in some countries you do this when you first meet someone

gte **t**oeehgtr - (n/v) a casual meeting of friends or family

itiroontcnud - (n) when two people you know meet for the first time, make an

_____

bdlni **d**tae - (n) a romantic meeting between two people who have never met before

frisidhnep - (n) if you are friends with someone you have one of these

hgna **o**tu - (v) an informal way of saying *spend time* with someone

senlgi - (adj) people who aren't in a relationship are this

Idioms and collocations

Let's go to the pub after the meeting, it will help *break the* _____ .

Wear your new tie to the job interview, it's important to make a good *first* _____ .

His new flatmate is as crazy as him, I think they'll *get on like a* _____ *on fire.*

Lisa is my best friend, in fact she's more than that, she's my _____ *mate.*

I think they will get on very well, they seem to have a lot *in* _____ .

soul	house	impression	common	ice

Grammar bit

<u>I work</u> in the marketing department of a large e-commerce company. <u>I write</u> press releases and <u>promote</u> our brand through Twitter and Facebook. At the moment <u>I'm working</u> on a project to increase our email mailing list.

17 Getting to know each other

What object would you rescue if your house was on fire ?	What kind of music do you listen to?
What do you watch on TV?	What was the last book you read?
Do you play any sports?	Where did you last go on holiday?
Do you have a favourite sports team?	What countries have you visited?
Have you lived in another city or country?	Who would you most like to meet?

18 Halloween

"I love horror movies. I mean, who doesn't like a good horror movie every once in a while? It's fun to get scared."
— Tara Reid

Mixed up vocabulary

stoknele - (n) the bone structure of an animal

nihatrgme - (n) a very bad dream

brsmtociok - (n) witches ride around on these

tdrerifei - (adj) how you would probably feel if you saw a ghost or a monster

cymeeret - (n) where dead people are buried

hrrroo **m**iveo - (n) a film designed to make you scared

vparmei - (n) a person who sucks your blood and steals your life energy

Idioms and collocations

The dog jumped onto the bed while I was sleeping and nearly *scared me to* _____ .

My neighbour *gives me the* _____ , he's always peeping out of his window.

The new sales manager is too perfect, she must have some _____ *in her closet.*

I don't like either candidate, but I suppose Smith is the *the lesser of two* _____ .

The search for the cause of the tragedy is in danger of becoming a _____ *hunt.*

evils   skeletons   witch   death   creeps

Grammar bit

"Is <u>anybody</u> there?", we asked the ouija board. Nothing happened. Suddenly <u>somebody</u> coughed and I jumped. Just then the doorbell rang and Tommy went to answer it. He came back looking as white as a ghost. "There was <u>nobody</u> there", he said.

18 Halloween

Do people celebrate Halloween in your country? How?	Do you believe in ghosts?
What's the scariest movie you've seen?	Do you like watching horror movies or reading horror novels?
What were you afraid of when you were a child?	Have you ever experienced something you couldn't explain?
Do you have any phobias?	Who would you like to put a curse on?
How superstitious are you?	Have you ever dressed up for halloween?

19 Health

"Sorry, there´s no magic bullet. You gotta eat healthy and live healthy to be healthy and look healthy. End of story."
— Morgan Spurlock

Mixed up vocabulary

wokr **o**tu - (n/v) a good hard session of physical activity

bladanec **d**eti - (n) eat the right amount of everything and not too much of anything

ercesexi - (n/v) another word for physical activity

bda **h**absti - (n) smoking, drinking, and eating too much sugar are examples of these

jkun **f**odo - (n) food with little nutritional value

ckehc **up** - (n/v) you should go to the doctor at least once a year for one of these

mnidecei - (n) if you are sick the doctor might tell you to take some of this

Idioms and collocations

My husband is such a *couch* _____ , he just watches TV and eats cookies.

After two months in a hospital bed, it's really great to be *back on my* _____ .

The stress was so bad in my last job that I almost had a *nervous* _____ .

You really should work fewer hours and try to get more sleep or you'll _____ *out.*

I didn't get the job, and to *rub* _____ *in the wound* my ex-assistant got it.

salt	*potato*	*feet*	*breakdown*	*burn*

Grammar bit

I'm so unfit these days. <u>I used to play</u> football twice a week and go swimming every weekend, <u>I didn't use to drive</u> everywhere, and <u>I always used to take</u> the stairs instead of the elevator.

19 Health

Do you have a healthy diet?	Do you get enough exercise?
What food or drinks do you avoid for health reasons?	Do you take vitamins or other supplements?
Do you try to take care of your brain as well as your body?	What's the biggest thing you could do to improve your health?
How often do you go to the doctor for a check-up?	Do you think people today are healthier or unhealthier than 50 years ago?
Are you allergic to anything?	How much sleep do you usually get? Is it enough?

20 Holidays

"I hate vacations. I hate them. I have no fun on them. I get nothing done. People sit and relax, but I don't want to relax. I want to see something."
— Paul Theroux

Mixed up vocabulary

srueoinv - (n) something you bring back from your holiday to help you remember it

lgeguga - (n) all the bags you take with you on holiday

exircneeeps - (n) you have these on holiday, good and bad

tvlrae **a**egtn - (n) a person who helps you to arrange a holiday

cmap s**e**ti - (n) somewhere you can pitch your tent

gddieu **t**ruo - (n) to be shown around an interesting place by an expert

go **s**intgseheig - (v) to take a look at the most famous and noteworthy places somewhere

Idioms and collocations

I'm really looking forward to the *day* _____ to Napoleon's birthplace tomorrow.

We stayed in a cosy little *bed and* _____ by the seaside.

If you _____ *in advance* you can get some really good deals.

The Niagara Falls is Canada's most visited *tourist* _____.

Don't pack too much! Last time you brought *everything but the kitchen* _____.

breakfast	*sink*	*attraction*	*trip*	*book*

Grammar bit

<u>Everything</u> about the holiday was wonderful. <u>Everyday</u> was warm and sunny and <u>all</u> the activities were fun and enjoyable. <u>Everybody</u> had a good time and they were sorry to have to leave.

20 Holidays

Have you ever stayed at a really nice hotel?	Where did you go for your last holiday?
What would be your dream holiday?	What kind of souvenirs do you bring back from your holidays?
Have you been or would you like to go on a cruise?	Do you try to learn a little of the language before holidaying abroad?
Would you like to live somewhere that you have visited on holiday?	What tips would you give holidaymakers who came to visit your town?
What was your worst holiday?	Do you know where your next holiday will be?

Home

"Any woman who understands the problems of running a home will be nearer to understanding the problems of running a country."
— Margaret Thatcher

Mixed up vocabulary

datercoe - (v) to freshen up a room or change its style

fruneruti - (n) tables, chairs, sideboard, cabinet, coffee table

acitt - (n) a room in the roof of a building

bcloyna - (n) on a nice day you can sit here and enjoy the sun

sodiut - (n) an apartment with only one main room

caerll - (n) a storage space under a building

monnsia - (n) a large and impressive house, often in the country

Idioms and collocations

It's so good to be back, there's *no _____ like home.*

My flat is very nice, but it's tiny. There *isn't enough room to swing a _____.*

Be careful what you say around here, *walls have _____.*

At least we have *a _____ over our heads* and food on the table.

I know it's tough, but *if you can't stand the heat get out of the _____.*

ears	kitchen	place	roof	cat

Grammar bit

I'm looking forward to moving out of my parents' home and having <u>my own room</u>. I'll do all <u>my own cooking</u> and washing and I'll decorate it <u>by myself</u>. I'll need some help moving though, I can't do that <u>on my own</u>.

21 Home

Is it better to buy than to rent?	How would you describe the style of your home?
What pictures do you have on your walls?	What's more important, comfort or style?
What's your favourite item of furniture?	Where and what would be your dream home?
What's your favourite spot in your home?	How many different places have you lived?
Do you get on well with your neighbours?	How long have you lived in your current home?

22 Humour

"The human race has only one really effective weapon and that is laughter."
— Mark Twain

Mixed up vocabulary

ceonmida - (n) a person who stands on a stage and tells jokes

soopf - (adj/n) a funny version of something serious

imirsosepn - (n) to do an i_____ is to pretend to be someone else for fun

ggilge - (n/v) a little laugh

foilsoh - (adj) something that isn't sensible

laaulbhge - (adj) total nonsense, completely unrealistic, hard to take seriously

cyrza - (adj) not normal, very unusual, mentally unbalanced

Idioms and collocations

It was difficult *keeping a straight* _____ when she told me about her incontinent

cat.

When he told me he'd bought a Ferrari, I didn't know whether *to laugh or to*

_____.

The show was so funny, I was *in* _____ from the beginning to the end.

Young man, stealing a policeman's helmet is *no laughing* _____!

Don't worry, the boss doesn't really want to see you, I was *playing a*_____ on you.

trick   cry   matter   stitches   face

Grammar bit

A guy says to his friend, "guess how many coins I have in my pocket."
The friends says, "<u>if I guess</u> right, <u>will you give</u> me one of them?"
The first guys says, "<u>if you guess</u> right, <u>I'll give</u> you both of them!"

22 Humour

What makes you laugh?	Can you think of a funny film you have seen?
Do you like to tell jokes?	Have you ever laughed at an inappropriate time?
Do you ever go to stand-up comedy shows?	Have you ever played a trick on anyone?
Have you ever read a book which made you laugh out loud?	Are there any English words which you find amusing?
Who is the funniest person you know?	What's the funniest TV show?

23 The internet

"The problem with the Internet is that it gives you everything - reliable material and crazy material. So the problem becomes, how do you discriminate?"
— Umberto Eco

Mixed up vocabulary

sioalc **n**ektwro - (n) websites like Facebook, Twitter and Instagram

bsoerrw - (n) an application you use to surf the internet

bdbranoad - (n) high speed internet

fyeurtelqn **a**kdes **q**toeuinss - (n) try checking these if you're looking for information

umrnesea - (n) you will need this and a password to log in to some sites

cdulo - (n) a non-local storage place where you can keep data

wseriesl **h**ootpts - (n) you can connect to the internet if you're near to one of these

Internet abbreviations

Be careful what you click on, some of those images are _____.

_____ , I just want to make myself a quick coffee.

_____ , Mike seems like a nice guy and has a lot of experience.

I know what you mean but _____ Sarah's better qualified and has great references.

_____ that puppy is hilarious!

OTOH   IMHO   LOL   BRB   NSFW

Grammar bit

<u>Despite</u> being less than 15 years old, Google has come to dominate the internet and become one of the world's biggest and most profitable companies <u>even though</u> most of its best known products are free to use.

23 The internet

Which websites do you visit the most?	**How much time do you spend on the internet?**
When did you first get on the internet?	**How worried are you about giving websites personal information?**
Have you ever created your own website?	**How has the internet affected your work?**
Do you think the internet should be more regulated?	**How do you think the internet might develop in the future?**
Do you ever shop online?	**What annoys you about the internet?**

24 Jobs

"I don't get out of bed for less than $10,000 a day"
— Linda Evangilista

Mixed up vocabulary

traenei - (n) a person who is learning how to do a job

jbo **i**eetrinwv - (n) you usually have one of these before you get a job

hamun **r**rueossce - (n) the department which recruits staff

sefl **e**ymdleop - (adj) if you work for yourself

fdrei - (v) if you make a big mistake at work, you might get this

unlodempye - (adj) to be out of work

craree - (n) a profession that you are in for a long time

Idioms and collocations

It's a _____ *job but someone's got to do it*

The best thing about being a teacher is I get real *job* _____ from helping my students.

Why are you still working in the supermarket doing that _____ *-end job?*

Rex, this cake you made isn't bad, but *don't give up the* _____ *job.*

I *got the* _____ from my last job, it was the best thing that ever happened to me.

satisfaction	*dirty*	*sack*	*dead*	*day*

Grammar bit

<u>I've been working</u> at PayMate.com for three years, and <u>I've been</u> in the Human Resources department for six months. Before <u>I came</u> here, <u>I worked</u> for an insurance company. <u>I've worked</u> for seven different companies in my life, so far.

24 Jobs

What was your first job?	What would be your dream job?
What's the worst job you've had?	What do you like about your job?
How will your job change in the future?	Do you know anyone with an interesting or unusual job?
If you won a lot of money, would you give up work?	How long have you had your current job?
What kind of job would you hate to have?	What do/did your parents do?

25 Law

"Laws are spider webs through which the big flies pass and the little ones get caught."
— Honoré de Balzac

Mixed up vocabulary

jeudg - (n/v) a person who makes important legal decisions

crotu **c**sea - (n) the process of resolving a legal issue

lawrye - (n) a person whose job it is to help with legal matters

wntsise - (n/v) a person who saw a crime happening

vdrtice - (n) a legal decision - guilty or not guilty

eicenved - (n) this is used to help prove someone's guilt or innocence

pinsro - (n) if you are found guilty, you may have to spend some time here

Idioms and collocations

If I don't get my money by Friday, I'm *taking you to* _____ .

The evidence looks bad, but we must remember he is *innocent until proven* _____ .

It's difficult to get a job if you have a *criminal* _____ .

The policeman was suspended from his job *under* _____ of taking bribes.

When the diamond was stolen, Lex Luthor was suspected of *committing the* _____

.

suspicion	court	crime	record	guilty

Grammar bit

The judge said that <u>as long as</u> Jones stayed away from his former boss's home and <u>provided that</u> he paid compensation for the damaged car, he would avoid going to jail. The judge said, "<u>Unless</u> you change your ways, I fear you will become a frequent visitor to this court".

25 Law

Which law should be abolished?	Is it ok to break the law sometimes?
What law would you like to introduce?	Have you ever got into trouble for breaking the law?
How much do you agree that there is one law for the rich and another for the poor?	What would you do if you found out that your company was breaking the law?
Would you like to be a police officer?	Do you think there should be more or fewer laws?
Have you ever visited a court?	Have you ever needed a lawyer?

26 Love and marriage

"Men marry women with the hope they will never change. Women marry men with the hope they will change. Usually they are both disappointed."
— Albert Einstein

Mixed up vocabulary

hyeononmo - (n) a holiday which couples have after getting married

rcantiom - (adj) a candlelight dinner could be described as this

dervciod - (adj) your marital status after you split from your husband or wife

ariaff - (n) a secret relationship

eaggned - (adj) after deciding to get married you are _____

meak a **c**ottmeinmm - (n) to promise to be loyal to someone (or something)

Idioms and collocations

Our eyes met across the room, it was *love at first* _____ .

My first wife and I _____ *up* after she had an affair with her boss.

Finally, he went *down on one* _____ and *popped the* _____ .

The actress's marriage is *on the* _____ after Brad was seen with a mystery woman.

After going out for five years, we decided to *tie the* _____ .

question	knee	rocks	knot	split	sight

Grammar bit

My wife, <u>who</u> I met on the top deck of a bus, has always been my best friend. Our garden, <u>where</u> we have recently installed a swimming pool, is the focus of our home life. Only my motorbike, <u>which</u> I ride every weekend, can drag me away from family life.

26 Love and marriage

What's the best thing about being in a relationship?	What's the best thing about being single?
Have you ever been on a date that didn't go well?	If you have a partner, how did you meet them?
Do you like weddings?	How romantic are you?
Would you ever use an online dating site?	What kind of people are you attracted to?
What are weddings like in your country?	Do you think couples should live together before getting married?

27 Money

"Too many people spend money they earned..to buy things they don't want..to impress people that they don't like."
— Will Rogers

Mixed up vocabulary

ccynrreu - (n) dollar, yen, euro, pound ...

wllate - (n) where men keep their money

tsrfearn - (v/n) to move money from one place to another

wtirawhd - (v) to take money out of a bank

bank accuton - (n) a safe place to keep your money

svsagni - (n) the money you don't spend

reetpci - (n) when you buy something you're usually given one of these

Idioms and collocations

I used to spend all my _____ *money* on sweets and comics.

He *made a* _____ selling bits of the Berlin wall to tourists.

Don't buy that solar iPhone case, it's a complete _____ *of money*.

This TV *cost an arm and a* _____ , but it was *worth every* _____ .

My last company *went* _____ after the accountant ran off with all the money.

fortune	*waste*	*pocket*	*leg*	*bankrupt*	*penny*

Grammar bit

I <u>should have put</u> my money on Turkish Nights, then I <u>would have won</u> more than £2,000.

 - Yes, we <u>could have had</u> a nice holiday with the money, and bought a new sofa.

27 Money

What professions are overpaid and underpaid?	What do you enjoy spending money on?
What have you bought today?	If you won a lot of money, what would you spend it on?
How many currencies can you name?	Do you prefer to pay by cash or plastic (credit/debit card)?
Did you get pocket money when you were a child?	What do you do with your small change?
Are you a saver or a spender?	Do you ever gamble?

28 Movies

"I have been a film buff all my life and believe that the finest cinema is fully the equal of the best novels."
— Salman Rushdie

Mixed up vocabulary

drtceoir - (n) the person in charge on a movie set

cats - (n/v) the actors in a movie

vnialil - (n) another word for *bad guy*

cosmute - (n) special clothes which the actors wear

flsakcbah - (n/v) a film scene which shows something happening in the past

telhilrr - (n) a movie with a lot of excitement and action

tarelri - (n) a preview of a film which is being released soon

Idioms and collocations

Call me old fashioned, but I like a film with a *happy* _____ .

The plot was predictable and the acting was bad, but the *special* _____ were amazing.

The movie of the book will be coming to the *big* _____ sometime in September.

It's amazing to think that the film is based on a *true* _____ .

An action movie isn't complete without big explosions and a *car* _____ .

chase   ending   story   effects   screen

Grammar bit

You <u>must</u> see the new X-Men film, it's really amazing, and you <u>have to</u> see it at the cinema on a big screen. Oh, and if you go on Tuesdays you <u>don't have to</u> pay full-price if you have a student card.

28 Movies

What was the last film you saw?	**Who is a famous actor from your country?**
Can you remember the first film you saw at the cinema?	**What film have you seen the most times?**
Do you like old black and white movies?	**Have you ever cried watching a movie?**
What kind of films don't you like?	**Have you ever walked out of a movie?**
Do you have a film collection?	**Who are your favourite actors?**

29 Music

"Music can change the world because it can change people."

— Bono

Mixed up vocabulary

vyiln - (n/adj) before MP3s, before CDs, before tape cassettes there was _____

csclailas - (adj) how we describe some European music from the 18th and 19th century

lisycr - (n) the words of a song

gerne - (n) pop, jazz, funk, soul and classical are all musical _____s

sdotiu - (n) where musicians record their music

centroc - (n) a musical performance for an audience

dermrum- (n) the musician who gives the music a beat

Idioms and collocations

This is such a *catchy* _____ , I can't stop singing it.

Angel was a *big* _____ for Robbie Williams in the mid nineties.

It's not looking good for the England team, but *it's not over until the fat* _____

sings.

The new ballad from Joss Stone is a real *tear-*_____ .

One hit _____ Joe Dolce spent three weeks at number one in 1981.

lady   jerker   tune   wonder   hit

Grammar bit

She has such a <u>beautiful</u> voice, and she sings especially <u>beautifully</u> on this album. The guitarist is really <u>good,</u> and the bassist plays <u>well</u> too. The whole band play <u>hard</u> and <u>fast</u> on this album.

29 Music

Who is a singer that you like?	What kind of music do you like?
How has your music taste changed as you've got older?	Are there any types of music you don't enjoy?
What's the best concert you've been to?	What was the best decade for pop music?
What was the first single or album that you bought?	Do you like modern pop music? Who do you like?
How often do you buy music? Where do you buy it from?	How do you discover new music?

30 Politics

"Anyone who is capable of getting themselves made President should on no account be allowed to do the job."
— Douglas Adams

Mixed up vocabulary

eictonle - (n) a chance to vote for your favourite politician

pyrat - (n) a political group

oinpion **p**llo - (n) a survey of potential voters' opinions

ftorn **r**eunrn - (n) the person who is winning in an election campaign

mrjioayt - (n/adj) more than 50%

debeat - (n) a discussion between political candidates

plicoy - (n) what a party plans/promises to do when they are in power

Idioms and collocations

It was a long and dirty *election* _____ which divided the country.

The Conservatives won a *landslide* _____ in the last general election.

I usually *cast my* _____ for the candidate who is more business friendly.

The problem with *two* _____ *systems* like in the US, is not all views are represented.

I'm a typical *floating* _____ , I never decide how to vote until the day of the election.

campaign victory vote party voter

Grammar bit

If you elect me for President, I promise I will make a difference. I will lower taxes for every citizen and I will make sure that every worker gets a fair deal. I will not stand by and watch the poor get poorer and the rich get richer.

30 Politics

How long is a political term in your country?	**Do you think you would be a good politician?**
Do you think it's important to vote?	**Who are the main political parties in your country?**
What makes a good politician?	**Are you interested in politics?**
Do you have similar political views to your parents?	**How much influence does the media have on people's political views?**
Do you have friends with different political views to you?	**If you were elected leader of your country, what law would you change first?**

31 School days

"The philosophy of the school room in one generation will be the philosophy of government in the next."
— Abraham Lincoln

Mixed up vocabulary

hdae **t**rahece - (n) the manager of a school

cmiucrrulu - (n) a detailed list of what is taught in school

sooclh **r**luse - (n) no chatting, don't chew gum, no mobile phones, wear grey trousers ...

bulyl - (n) a person who physically or verbally abuses another person

sjbtceu - (n) English, Maths, Geography, Biology, Chemistry, Computer Studies ...

erexcise **b**oko - (n) what students write in at school

setsreem - (n) the school year is usually divided into three of these

Idioms and collocations

I was *teacher's* _____ at school, I always had my hand up first, always got a gold star.

At school there was a prize for the students who got *top* _____ in Maths and English.

If she's late again, we'll go without her. That will *teach her a* _____ .

English was so boring! We had to learn all these old poems *off by* _____ , I hated it.

The worst thing you could do at school was *tell* _____ on the other students.

heart   lesson   tales   marks   pet

Grammar bit

My favourite teacher was Dr. Gardner, our History teacher. <u>He was always making</u> bad jokes and <u>he would sometimes bring</u> in movies to watch in the class.

31 School days

What were your favourite subjects at school?	**Who was your favourite teacher?**
Were any of your teachers a bit strange?	**How did you get to school?**
Do you agree that "school days are the best days of your life"?	**What did you use to do at break time?**
Were you a good school pupil or a bit naughty?	**Did you have to wear a school uniform? What was it?**
Was bullying a problem at your school?	**What should school children be taught to help prepare them for "the real world"?**

32 Shopping

"The odds of going to the store for a loaf of bread and coming out with only a loaf of bread are three billion to one."
— Erma Bombeck

Mixed up vocabulary

dtamnerpet **s**rteo - (n) a shop where you can buy a wide range of products

gsocrreei - (n) everyday shopping such as food, cleaning items, cat food, etc.

chgainng **r**omo - (n) a place where you can try on clothes before buying them

bganira - (n/v) an item selling at a very good price

reundf - (n/v) if you return an item to a shop, they should give you one of these

gfti **v**cehuro - (n) it's similar to money but you can only spend it in one shop

mnnanqiue - (n) a lifesize model of a person which is used for displaying clothes

Idioms and collocations

I haven't got any money, but we can go uptown and do some _____ *shopping.*

We're going to Milan for the weekend, and we're going to *shop until we* _____.

I had *buyer's* _____ after spending $300 on a pair of Italian shoes.

Don't let the dog go in Grandma's living room, he's like a _____ *in a china shop.*

Buy now, pay later! Get *interest free* _____ on all purchases made in September.

credit   window   drop   remorse   bull

Grammar bit

Is that the time? <u>I'm going to be</u> late! <u>I'm meeting</u> Cheryl at the mall. <u>We're going to look</u> at dresses for Kylie's wedding. <u>She's getting</u> married next month.

32 Shopping

Do you have a favourite shop?	What do you enjoy shopping for?
Do you shop online?	Have you ever suffered from buyer's remorse?
Do you prefer to shop alone or with friends?	What's the best place for shopping in your town or city?
How often do you buy clothes?	Where do you buy your groceries?
Have you ever worked in a shop?	What's the worst thing about shopping?

33 Sleep

"Have you ever noticed that the word bed looks like one."

— Andrew Berlin

Mixed up vocabulary

negtiamrh - (n) a bad dream

pollwi - (n) what you rest your head on in bed

bnuk bde - (n) two beds stacked on top of each other

sroen - (v/n) a noise some people make while they sleep

beisded tbela - (n) a piece of furniture next to the bed

sipgnele pisll - (n) a doctor might give you these to help you sleep

bkanelt - (n) put this on your bed to help you keep warm at night

Idioms and collocations

Night _____ *, sweet* _____ *,* see you in the morning.

I must have been tired, I *slept like a* _____ last night.

I didn't sleep well, I *tossed and* _____ all night.

I know it's a big decision, _____ *on it* and give me an answer in the morning.

I usually *have a* _____ when I get home before I start preparing dinner.

log	*nap*	*dreams*	*sleep*	*turned*	*night*

Grammar bit

I <u>was lying</u> in bed reading when I heard a noise. I called to my wife <u>who was cleaning</u> her teeth in the bathroom and told her to lock the door. The noise <u>was coming</u> from downstairs so I grabbed a torch and a heavy ornament and went to investigate.

33 Sleep

How many hours sleep do you need? How many do you normally get?	**Do you or your partner snore?**
How long does it take you to fall asleep?	**What do you do if you can't sleep?**
Can you usually remember your dreams?	**Are you a heavy or a light sleeper?**
Do you spring out of bed in the morning, or do you need more time to wake up?	**What's the first thing you do when you wake up?**
What position do you like to sleep in?	**Do you read or watch TV in bed?**

34 Sport

"Football is a simple game. Twenty-two men chase a ball for 90 minutes and at the end, the Germans always win."

— Gary Lineker

Mixed up vocabulary

rtkcae - (n) you need one of these to play tennis

tmnrutaoen - (n) a sporting competition

seim flian - (n) the last four competitors meet in one of these

tyhrop - (n) the winner(s) of a competition are presented with one of these

rreefee - (n) a person who makes sure the rules of the sport are followed

chnoiapm - (n) the winner of a sporting competition

pltaeyn - (n) a punishment for breaking the rules of a sport

Idioms and collocations

They ran out of time before it was my turn to speak, I was really *saved by the*

_____.

The Republican candidate is ten points behind and seems to be *on the* _____.

Ok Sandra, can you *get the* _____ *rolling* and tell us how you got on last week.

I think it's *a safe* _____ that my contract will be extended for another year.

Well, we've sent them our proposal, *the ball's in their* _____ now.

ball	bet	bell	court	ropes

Grammar bit

Manchester <u>haven't been</u> beaten <u>for</u> almost 100 games and they <u>haven't lost</u> to this team <u>since</u> 1961. In fact these two teams <u>haven't met</u> <u>for</u> more than two decades, not <u>since</u> that classic semi-final match in 1993.

34 Sport

What sports do you like to watch?	Do you play any sports?
Which sportsmen and women do you admire?	If you could play any sport professionally, which sport would you choose?
Do you ever go to watch live sporting events?	If you could watch any sporting event live, which event would you choose?
Do you support any sports teams?	Are there any sports you don't enjoy watching?
What are the most popular sports in your country?	Do you ever gamble on sporting events?

35 Technology

"Any sufficiently advanced technology is indistinguishable from magic."

— Arthur C. Clarke

Mixed up vocabulary

inennovti - (n) a useful new device or machine

deplove - (v) to make something new or more advanced

geagdt - (n) a small piece of equipment that does a specific job

fetuare - (n) a special function that a piece of equipment has

obetolse - (adj) something which is no longer used e.g. Betamax, Internet Explorer 3

potabrle - (adj) a piece of equipment which can be transported

brhoauktrgeh - (n) an important discovery which helps progress to be made

Idioms and collocations

The car has all the *bells and* _____ you would expect from a top of the range BMW.

I'm an *early* _____ , I bought the first iPhone the day it came out.

The Sony Playstation provided a *quantum* _____ forward in video game graphics.

These nifty graphics are created *on the* _____ by the processor.

I'm sure you can do it Jeff , *it's not* _____ *science.*

leap   adopter   fly   rocket   whistles

Grammar bit

So much <u>has changed</u> in my lifetime. When I was a boy <u>we didn't use to have</u> a telephone and <u>we had to use</u> the phone box on the corner. Now I can have a video chat with friends in Australia at any time for free. <u>I haven't used</u> a phone box for 20 years.

35 Technology

What's the most advanced piece of technology that you own?	Are you excited by new technology?
Do you think people rely too much on technology nowadays?	Do you find any modern gadgets frustrating to use?
What modern gadget could you not live without?	Would you like to own a robot that did most of the housework?
What do you think has been the most important invention in your lifetime?	Do you own any technology that is now obsolete?
Are you an early adopter or do you like to wait until something has been tried and tested before buying it?	Are you concerned about any new or imminent technologies?

36 Television

"I have never seen a bad television program, because I refuse to. God gave me a mind, and a wrist that turns things off."
— Jack Paar

Mixed up vocabulary

s**ti-c**mo - (n) a funny TV show featuring the same characters every week

tkal **s**hwo - (n) a program where the host interviews interesting guests

rmteoe **c**toonlr - (n) a device for changing TV channels from the sofa

eediops - (n) a single show in a TV series

pretreens - (n) another name for a person who fronts a TV show

ftal **s**enrec - (adj/n) most televisions sold today have one of these

cammcrielo - (n) a short program that tries to sell you a product or service

Idioms and collocations

Is there anything good *on the* _____ tonight?

I'm going camping tomorrow, so I want to see the _____ *forecast.*

Have a look in the *TV* _____ and see if there are any good films on later.

I don't watch TV much nowadays, there's too much _____ *and violence* for me.

I don't usually go out on Friday evenings, I like to _____ *out* in front of the TV.

chill   sex   guide   box   weather

Grammar bit

I <u>put</u> the kettle <u>on</u> to make a cup of tea and <u>turned on</u> the TV to watch the football. Unfortunately, the match was <u>called off</u> because of bad weather so I <u>turned</u> the TV <u>off</u> and <u>put on</u> some music.

36 Television

What was your favourite TV show when you were a child?	**What TV channel do you watch the most?**
Do you watch any reality TV shows?	**What are the most popular TV shows in your country?**
Do you ever stream or download shows from the internet?	**Do you watch any soap operas?**
In your opinion, what are some of the best TV shows ever made?	**How do you decide what to watch on TV?**
Can you remember being shocked by a television programme?	**Who are your favourite and least favourite TV presenters?**

37 Time

"Yesterday's the past, tomorrow's the future, but today is a gift. That's why it's called the present."
— Bil Keane

Mixed up vocabulary

hroiyts - (n) everything that has happened up to now

cunetyr - (n) one hundred years

lape **y**rae - (n) February 29 occurs in one of these

fgrihtont - (n) two weeks

mtghidin - (n) 00:00

dceeda - (n) ten years

mmteon - (n) a very short period of time

Idioms and collocations

Gosh, is it midnight already? How *time flies when you're having* _____.

In the long _____ the interest rate rise could have a major effect on the economy.

I spent all day trying to get my printer working, it was a complete _____ *of time.*

I took a taxi to the venue and got there *just in* _____ to see the first band.

I hardly ever see my old school friends, *once in a blue* _____ we meet up for a drink.

time	moon	fun	term	waste

Grammar bit

I spend <u>too much time</u> at work and <u>too little time</u> on doing the housework. There's <u>never enough time</u> to get all the little jobs done, it <u>takes so long</u> to get the house nice and clean.

37 Time

Do you wear a watch?	If you could freeze time, what would you do?
If you had more free time, how would you spend it?	Are you good at managing your time?
What do you consider to be a waste of time?	What time-saving gadget do you wish someone would invent?
When does time go quickly or slowly for you?	When was the best time of your life?
Are you usually on time for events and appointments?	If you had a time machine, which period would you visit?

38 Towns and cities

"Happiness is having a large, loving, caring, close-knit family in another city."
— George Burns

Mixed up vocabulary

sbbrsuu - (n) the housing area outside of the main city

satmidu - (n) where sporting events take place

nihtifgel - (n) evening entertainment

comalopostin - (adj) an interesting mix of cultures and lifestyles

fael makert - (n) a place where you can buy second hand things

senilyk - (n) the outline of a city, Hong Kong and New York's are both impressive

cneltra snotati - (n) the main terminal for catching trains

Idioms and collocations

I'm thinking of moving to a more *up and* _____ area of the city.

I'm not a city person, I prefer the *peace and* _____ of the countryside.

Sorry I'm late, I got stuck in a *traffic* _____ on the other side of town.

It's not a good area for children, the _____ *rate* is quite high.

The city has great *public* _____ , you don't really need a car.

jam	coming	transport	crime	quiet

Grammar bit

I have so much to do before the wedding. I have to <u>get my hair done</u> at the salon and then I need to <u>get my nails manicured</u>. I'm <u>having my dress altered</u> so I need to pick that up and I need to <u>get my shoes mended</u> too.

38 Towns and cities

If you had to give some visitors a tour of your hometown, what would you show them?	What do you like to do when you visit a new town or city?
What do you like about the town or city where you live now?	What would improve your town or city?
If you could live in any city, where would you choose?	Would you prefer to live in the city or the country?
Are there "good" and "bad" parts of your town?	What is your hometown famous for?
Is your town changing? In what ways?	What's your favourite part of town?

39 Travel

"You go away? So that you can come back. So that you can see the place you came from with new eyes and extra colors. Coming back to where you started is not the same as never leaving."
— Terry Pratchett

Mixed up vocabulary

denaostiitn - (n) the place you are traveling to

daertp - (v) another word for *leave*

shulett **b**su - (n) one of these will take you from the airport to the hotel

oen **w**ya **t**itcek - (n) buy one of these if you're not planning on coming back

tavler **i**rscenaun - (n) this covers things like theft, cancellations and medical care

rayunw - (n) a plane uses one of these when it takes off and lands

hnad **l**egguag - (n) you can take this onto a plane, but not too much

Idioms and collocations

We don't like to travel to touristy places, we prefer to get *off the beaten* _____.

I wish I'd bought shares in Apple last year, I think I've *missed the* _____ now.

We might have to raise the price later, but we'll *cross that* _____ *when we get to it.*

I don't know what time the flight is, Sarah makes all the _____ *arrangements.*

I'm in Delhi on a *business* _____ next week, but maybe we can meet the week after.

trip	boat	track	bridge	travel

Grammar bit

<u>I'd better go</u> or I will miss my train. <u>I should try</u> and get to the station early so I can buy my family some presents and <u>I ought to get</u> something for my colleagues too.

39 Travel

What's your favourite city or country?	What countries have you visited?
What kind of places do you like to visit?	How do you use the internet when making travel plans?
What's the best or worst hotel you've stayed in?	Do you take a lot of luggage when you travel or do you travel light?
What's a memorable place you've visited?	Do you like traveling alone?
Which country or city would you most like to visit?	What do you like about traveling?

40 The unexplained

"Two possibilities exist: either we are alone in the Universe or we are not. Both are equally terrifying."
— Arthur C. Clarke

Mixed up vocabulary

myisetuors - (adj) unusual and unexplainable

suturnapreal - (adj/n) not explained by the laws of nature

arslogoty - (n) the belief that you can predict the future from the position of the planets

renianatricon - (n) the idea that people are born again in another body after they die

thaetlpey - (n) the ability to read the thoughts of another person

sciltepac - (adj) to be questioning or doubtful about a claim

cpronsyiac **t**reohy - (n) an explanation of an event which is different to the official version

Idioms and collocations

This old lady in Greece *told me my* _____ , she said I'd marry a beautiful doctor.

I thought I heard a noise downstairs and I _____ *out*. It was only my cat.

I love pizza and pasta! I think I must have been Italian *in a past* _____ .

That's very interesting if it's true, but I'll *take it with a pinch of* _____ .

Touch _____ , this time tomorrow the project will be finished and we can relax.

life   freaked   wood   fortune   salt

Grammar bit

<u>I've got to admit</u> this house is very spooky, I don't like it here at all.

- Yeah, <u>I've got to get going</u>, this place gives me the creeps.

40 The unexplained

Have you ever seen or experienced something you couldn't explain?	**Have you ever been hypnotised?**
Have you ever felt that you had a telepathic link with someone?	**What conspiracy theories do you believe could be true?**
Do you think humans have already made contact with extraterrestrial beings?	**What mysteries are connected with your town or country?**
Have you ever had a dream that came true?	**Do you think someone's star sign can affect their personality?**
What do you think about alternative medicines like acupuncture or homeopathy?	**How superstitious are you?**

41 The weather

"There's no such thing as bad weather, just soft people."
— Bill Bowerman

Mixed up vocabulary

huiracnre - (n) a very big storm

cyodlu - (adj) when it's like this, you can't see the blue sky or the sun

lthninigg - (n) a streak of electricity and light which you sometimes see during a storm

rownabi - (n) you might see one of these when it stops raining and the sun comes out

srhoew - (n) a short, hard period of rain

hdmui - (adj) when it's hot and the air is moist

pludde - (n) a small pool of water left after rainfall

Idioms and collocations

I'm going to go home, I'm feeling a bit *under the* _____ .

She's been on _____ *nine* since she got offered a place at university.

Tomorrow will be much busier, this is the *calm before the* _____ .

Hi honey! I'm going to be late home, I'm _____ *under* at the office.

Well, look on the *bright* _____ , at least we don't have to work at the weekend.

snowed   storm   side   cloud   weather

Grammar bit

<u>I wish I lived</u> somewhere warmer where it didn't rain so much.
 - Yeah, and <u>I wish I had packed</u> a jumper it's quite chilly tonight.

41 The weather

What's your favourite season?	What's your favourite kind of weather?
What do you like to do on a rainy Sunday?	Have you ever experienced extreme weather conditions?
Is it normal in your country to make small talk about the weather?	How many different words or phrases can you think of to describe rain in English?
What's your least favourite type of weather?	Have you ever thought about moving to a country with a different climate?
What are the hottest and coldest temperatures you have experienced?	Do you prefer winter clothes or summer clothes?

42 Xmas

"The two most joyous times of the year are Christmas morning and the end of school."
— Alice Cooper

Mixed up vocabulary

sngitcok - (n) Santa fills one of these with presents if you've been good

trkeuy - (n) British people often eat this for Christmas dinner

agenl - (n) one of these sits on top of the Christmas tree

reedenri - (n) an animal which helps pull Santa's sleigh

swmnona - (n) sometimes smokes a pipe and has a carrot for a nose

dcrtieasnoo - (n) things you put up to make a home feel more festive

atvend caaelrdn - (n) has 24 doors which are opened a day at a time

Idioms and Christmas songs

Come on, it's Christmas who wants a *kiss under the* _____*?*

Don't look a gift _____ *in the mouth,* take the money and no more questions.

I'm dreaming of a white _____ *, just like the ones I used to know.*

_____ *roasting on an open fire, Jack Frost nipping at your nose,*

Rudolph the red-nosed reindeer had a very shiny _____ *.*

nose	*mistletoe*	*horse*	*Christmas*	*chestnuts*

Grammar bit

Don't forget to <u>tidy up</u> your room, <u>hang up</u> your stocking, <u>leave out</u> some milk and cookies, <u>wrap up</u> your presents, and DON'T <u>get up</u> too early!

42 Xmas

What is a typical Christmas Day for you?	What do you like to eat at Christmas time?
Do you usually go to church at Christmas time?	Do you like Christmas music?
What do you dislike about Christmas?	Do you do your Christmas shopping nice and early or at the last minute?
Do you wish it could be Christmas every day?	Do you enjoy buying presents for other people?
What Christmas traditions do you enjoy?	Are there any special films or TV shows that you like to watch at Christmas?

43 Future with *will*

Use

To make predictions about the future
- *I'm sure Italy will beat Belgium in the semi-final*
- *The new hologram TVs probably won't be available until next year*

When we make spontaneous decisions
- *I'll have the steak please*
- *Hold on, I'll see if she's in her office*

To make promises or threats about future action
- *I promise I'll make it up to you*
- *I won't forget this*

Form

(+) subject + will + infinitive
(-) subject + will not (won't) + infinitive
(?) (question word) + will + subject + infinitive?

Mixed up sentences

Perhaps be park the sunny will tomorrow to go it can and we
I a have piece steak of for nice tonight dinner I'll think
I'll getting Nissan a Micra up probably end
England won't win definitely Brazil against
Maybe drivers will cars work put taxi out of self-driving

43 Future with *will*

Where will you be this time tomorrow?	**What will the world be like in 50 years?**
Who will win the next football (soccer) World Cup?	**How will you spend your time when you retire?**
Will people work more or less in the future?	**What will be your next big purchase?**
What features will the iPhone 20 have?	**Who will be the next President of the USA?**
Will people still carry cash in 20 years?	**When will flying cars be invented?**

44 & 45 Past simple

Use

To talk about completed actions which happened at a specific time in the past (although the specific time isn't always clearly stated)

- *I saw John this morning, he didn't look very happy*
- *Last year, we went to Vegas and had a really crazy time*

Form

(+) subject + past form + infinitive
(-) subject + did not + infinitive
(?) (question word) + did + subject + infinitive?

Mixed up sentences

In we bathrooms house two my had last

I answered I home you nobody when called but got

I when was in meditation I India into got

What time last did night? home get you

I to was go because party the too I didn't tired

44 Past simple: childhood

What games did you play in the school playground?	**Who were your best friends where you lived?**
What did you enjoy doing at school?	**What was your favourite toy?**
What did you use to spend your pocket money on?	**What TV shows did you enjoy?**
What pictures did you have on your bedroom walls?	**What's the first film you remember seeing at the cinema?**
What food didn't you use to like?	**What was it like where you lived?**

45 Past simple: recent past

What did you have for breakfast this morning?	**What was the last film you saw?**
Who did you last talk to on the telephone?	**What did you last read?**
What time did you go to bed last night?	**What did you watch on TV last night?**
What was the last photograph you took?	**When did you last see the sea?**
What did you buy yesterday?	**What was the last meal you cooked?**

46 Present continuous

Use

To talk about actions which are happening at the present moment.
- *I'm eating dinner can I call you back?*
- *What are you doing? You're making a lot of noise.*

The present moment can be interpreted as meaning today, this week, this time in my life, etc.
- *I'm reading a really good book at the moment*
- *I'm thinking of buying a house and moving to the country*

The *present continuous* is also used to talk about future arrangements.
- *I'm meeting Todd tomorrow*
- *We're spending a week in Krakow and then driving to Budapest*

Form

(+) subject + am/is/are + 'ing' form
(-) subject + am/is/are + not + 'ing' form
(?) (question word) + am/is/are + subject + 'ing' form

Mixed up sentences

I'm work printer this having to getting problems
I'm watching at brilliant the this TV moment show
Where you are these days? living
I'm to because later drinking not Munich I'm driving
We're next moving house new into our weekend

46 Present continuous

Are you reading a good book at the moment?	What are you having for dinner tonight?
What are you looking forward to?	What is a friend of yours probably doing at the moment?
What projects are you working on at home or at work right now?	What's happening in the news at the moment?
Where are you going after this class?	What are you wearing today?
How are your English classes going?	Why are you learning English?

47 & 48 Present perfect

Use

Present perfect is used to talk about actions which have or haven't happened and which have a <u>connection with the present</u>.

- *I've already eaten thank you, I'm really not hungry.*
- *Are you going to Disneyland? We've been there, we had a great time.*

Present perfect is also used to describe the state of things from a time in the past until the present

- *House prices have risen by 15% this year.*
- *I've lived in the same flat for 12 years.*

Form

(+) subject + have/has + past participle (3rd form)
(-) subject + have/has + not + past participle
(?) (question word) + have/has + subject + past participle

Mixed up sentences

I've seen James film a Bond never
Have London been to before? you
I've have him? my you husband, seen lost
I've Stephanie to idea she talked it's thinks a and great
We're celebrating university to been because Maria's accepted

47 Present perfect: have you ever ...?

Have you ever seen or met a celebrity?	Have you ever ridden a horse or other animal?
Have you ever locked yourself out of your house or car?	Have you ever got lost on holiday?
Have you ever walked out of a movie before it finished?	Have you ever been on TV?
Have you ever dreamt something that later came true?	Have you ever eaten an insect?
Have you ever missed a plane flight?	Have you ever had a bad haircut?

48 Present perfect: life history

What's the most disgusting thing you've eaten?	What's the longest journey you've ever been on?
What's the nicest hotel you've ever stayed at?	What's the most exciting activity you've ever done?
What's the nicest car you have ever travelled in?	What's the most exciting sporting event you have watched?
Which film have you watched the most times?	What's the worst job you've had?
How many places have you lived since you were born?	Have you ever bought something and regretted it later?

49 Present simple

Use

Present simple is mostly used to talk about general facts and routine actions. It is also used to talk about scheduled future events.

- *I usually start work at 8am and finish at 6pm. I never get home before 7pm*
- *Chelsea wear a blue strip and play at Stamford Bridge*
- *The train leaves at 3.30pm*

Form

(+) subject + infinitive(+s)
(-) subject + do not/does not + infinitive
(?) (question word) + do/does + subject + infinitive

Mixed up sentences

I town a small in in Wales live

John butcher works for local the

What think global warming? about you do

Jenny so doesn't flying travel by train we like

Do prefer Apple Macintosh? or use to an a you PC

49 Present simple

Where do you live?	**Where do you work?**
What do you do at the weekends?	**Who do you talk to the most?**
How often do you go to the cinema?	**How far from here do you live?**
How many pairs of shoes do you have?	**What time do you go to bed during the week?**
Why do you think English is important?	**How often do you get your hair cut?**

50 Second conditional

Use

The second conditional is used to describe unlikely or hypothetical situations

- *If we had a bigger car, I wouldn't have this problem*
- *I would go and see a doctor if I were you*
- *If I could live anywhere in the world, I would live in San Francisco*
- *What would you say if I told you I was getting married*

Form

if + subject + past form …, subject + would + infinitive … (or)

subject + would + infinitive … if + subject + past form …

Note: In second conditional sentences it is grammatically correct to use *were* instead of *was* in the *if clause*, although this rule is often ignored by native speakers.

Mixed up sentences

If to the chance, see I like Australia had I would

If probably she the she have children, take didn't would job

If I I your ask for advice, wanted it would

If more time, could features more had we add we

I mouth your if in I that you were put wouldn't

50 Second conditional

What country would you like to visit?	What would you do if you had more free time?
What would you do if you could turn invisible?	Where would you live if you could live anywhere?
If you could meet anyone alive or dead, who would you like to meet?	If you could change any law, what would you change?
If there were a pill that enabled you to live to 1000, would you take it?	If you had $1,000,000 to invest, how would you invest it?
How would you feel if the internet stopped working?	If you had to change jobs, what would you do instead?

Answer key

1

childhood, teenager, pensioner, middle-aged, mature, retirement, toddler

grows up, getting on a bit, good for your age, golden age, time of our lives

2

irritate, pest, inconvenient, frustrated, furious, bad mood, calm down

pain in the neck, driving me crazy, gets on my nerves, hit the roof, bugs me

3

vet, collar, hibernate, purr, mammal, reptile, bark

quiet as a mouse, black sheep, dog eat dog, eat a horse, let the cat out of the bag

4

paint, drawing, gallery, portrait, masterpiece, canvas, technique

a picture is worth a thousand words, judge a book by its cover, draw a line, paint the town red, back to the drawing board

5

presents, cake, candles, gift voucher, party, surprise, balloon

come of age, life of the party, have a ball, let your hair down, piece of cake

6

contents, chapter, plot, paperback, index, skim, non-fiction

in her good books, lost the plot, new chapter, truth is stranger than fiction, reading between the lines

7

marketing, manager, advertise, profit, loss, break even, meeting

keep me in the loop, take the minutes, meet the deadline, corner the market, got the green light

8

traffic jam, brake, reverse, windscreen, spare tyre, road sign, engine

driving me round the bend, change gear, dead end, in the driving seat, fasten your seatbelt

9

suit, underwear, wardrobe, tight, baggy, plain, heels

bores the pants off me, dressed to kill, got the boot, below the belt, roll up our sleeves

10

argument, ban, compromise, issue, abolish, point of view, debate

on my side, agreed to differ, heated debate, over her dead body, sitting on the fence

11

media, disaster, election, demonstration, award show, trivial, court case

hit the headlines, added fuel to the fire, in the same boat, once in a blue moon, a flash in the pan

12

check, main course, reservation, well done, vegetarian, cruelty, napkin

my treat, doggy bag, bigger than my belly, completely stuffed, sweet tooth

13

rain forest, boycott, countryside, wildlife, planet, pollute, slick

can't see the wood for the trees, not in my nature, tip of the iceberg, drop in the ocean, make a mountain out of a molehill

14

celebrity, red carpet, gossip, tabloid, star, glamorous, premier

down to earth, claim to fame, stage fright, in the headlines, front page news

15

nutritious, delicious, flavour, bland, recipe, texture, portion

bowl of cherries, cool as a cucumber, carrot and stick, not my cup of tea, in a nutshell

16

robot, prediction, fortune teller, forecast, utopia, apocalypse, breakthrough

ahead of its time, look into my crystal ball, educated guess, short term, time will tell

17

shake hands, get together, introduction, blind date, friendship, hang out, single

break the ice, first impression, get on like a house on fire, soul mate, in common

18

skeleton, nightmare, broomstick, terrified, horror movie, vampire

scared me to death, gives me the creeps, skeletons in her closet, the lesser of two evils, witch hunt

19

work out, balanced diet, exercise, bad habits, junk food, check up, medicine

couch potato, back on my feet, nervous breakdown, burn out, rub salt in the wound

20

souvenir, luggage, experience, travel agent, camp site, guided tour, go sightseeing

day trip, bed and breakfast, book in advance, tourist attraction, everything but the kitchen sink

21

decorate, furniture, attic, balcony, studio, cellar, mansion

no place like home, isn't enough room to swing a cat, walls have ears, a roof over our heads, if you can't stand the heat get out of the kitchen

22

comedian, spoof, impression, giggle, foolish, laughable, crazy

keeping a straight face, to laugh or to cry, in stitches, no laughing matter, playing a prank

23

social network, browser, broadband, frequently asked questions, username, cloud, wireless hotspot

Not Safe For Work, Be Right Back, In My Humble Opinion, On The Other Hand, Rolling On the Floor Laughing

24

trainee, job interview, human resources, self employed, fired, unemployed, career

it's a dirty job, job satisfaction, dead end job, don't give up the day job, got the sack

25

judge, court case, lawyer, witness, verdict, evidence, prison

taking you to court, innocent until proven guilty, criminal record, under suspicion, commiting the crime

26

honeymoon, romantic, divorced, affair, engaged, make a commitment

love at first sight, split up, down on one knee, popped the question, on the rocks, tie the knot

27

currency, wallet, transfer, withdraw, bank account, savings, receipt

pocket money, made a fortune, waste of money, an arm and a leg, worth every penny, went bankrupt

28

director, cast, villain, costume, flashback, thriller, trailer

happy ending, special effects, big screen, real life, car chase

29

vinyl, classical, lyrics, genre, studio, concert, drummer

catchy tune, big hit, it's not over until the fat lady sings, tear jerker, one hit wonder

30

election, party, opinion poll, front runner, majority, debate, policy

election campaign, landslide victory, cast my vote, two party system, floating voter

31

head teacher, curriculum, school rules, bully, subject, exercise book, semester
teacher's pet, top marks, teach her a lesson, off by heart, tell tales

32

department store, groceries, changing room, bargain, refund, gift voucher, mannequin
window shopping, shop until we drop, buyer's remorse, bull in a china shop, interest free credit

33

nightmare, pillow, bunk bed, snore, bedside table, sleeping pills, blanket
night night, sweet dreams, slept like a log, tossed and turned, sleep on it, have a nap

34

racket, tournament, semi final, trophy, referee, champion, penalty
saved by the bell, on the ropes, get the ball rolling, a safe bet, the ball's in their court

35

invention, develop, gadget, feature, obsolete, portable, breakthrough
bells and whistles, early adopter, quantum leap, on the fly, it's not rocket science

36

sit-com, talk show, remote control, episode, presenter, flat screen, commercial
on the box, weather forecast, TV guide, sex and violence, chill out

37

history, century, leap year, fortnight, midnight, decade, moment
time flies when you're having fun, in the long run, waste of time, just in time, once in a blue moon

38

suburbs, stadium, nightlife, cosmopolitan, flea market, skyline, central station
up and coming, peace and quiet, traffic jam, crime rate, public transport

39

destination, depart, shuttle bus, one way ticket, travel insurance, runway, hand luggage
off the beaten track, missed the boat, cross that bridge when we get to it, travel arrangements, business trip

40

mysterious, supernatural, astrology, reincarnation, telepathy, sceptical, conspiracy theory
told me my fortune, freaked out, in a past life, take it with a grain of salt, touch wood

41

hurricane, cloudy, lightning, rainbow, shower, humid, puddle
under the weather, cloud nine, calm before the storm, under the weather, bright side

42

stocking, turkey, angel, reindeer, snowman, decorations, advent calendar
kiss under the mistletoe, don't look a gift horse in the mouth, white christmas, chestnuts roasting, shiny nose

43

Perhaps it will be sunny tomorrow and we can go to the park
I think I'll have a nice piece of steak for dinner tonight
I'll probably end up getting a Nissan Micra
England definitely won't win against Brazil
Maybe self-driving cars will put taxi drivers out of work

44, 45

In my last house we had two bathrooms
I called you when I got home but nobody answered
I got into meditation when I was in India
What time did you get home last night?
I didn't go to the party because I was too tired

46

I'm having problems getting this printer to work
I'm watching this brilliant TV show at the moment
Where are you living these days?
I'm not drinking because I'm driving to Munich later
We're moving into our new house next weekend

47,48

I've never seen a James Bond film
Have you been to London before?
I've lost my husband, have you seen him?
I've talked to Stephanie and she thinks it's a great idea
Maria's been accepted to university so we're celebrating

49

I live in a small town in Wales
John works for the local butcher
What do you think about global warming?
Jenny doesn't like flying so we travel by train
Do you prefer to use a PC or an Apple Macintosh?

50

If I had the chance, I would like to see Australia

If she didn't have children, she would probably take the job

If I wanted your advice, I would ask for it

If we had more time, we could add more features

I wouldn't put that in your mouth if I were you

Printed in Great Britain
by Amazon